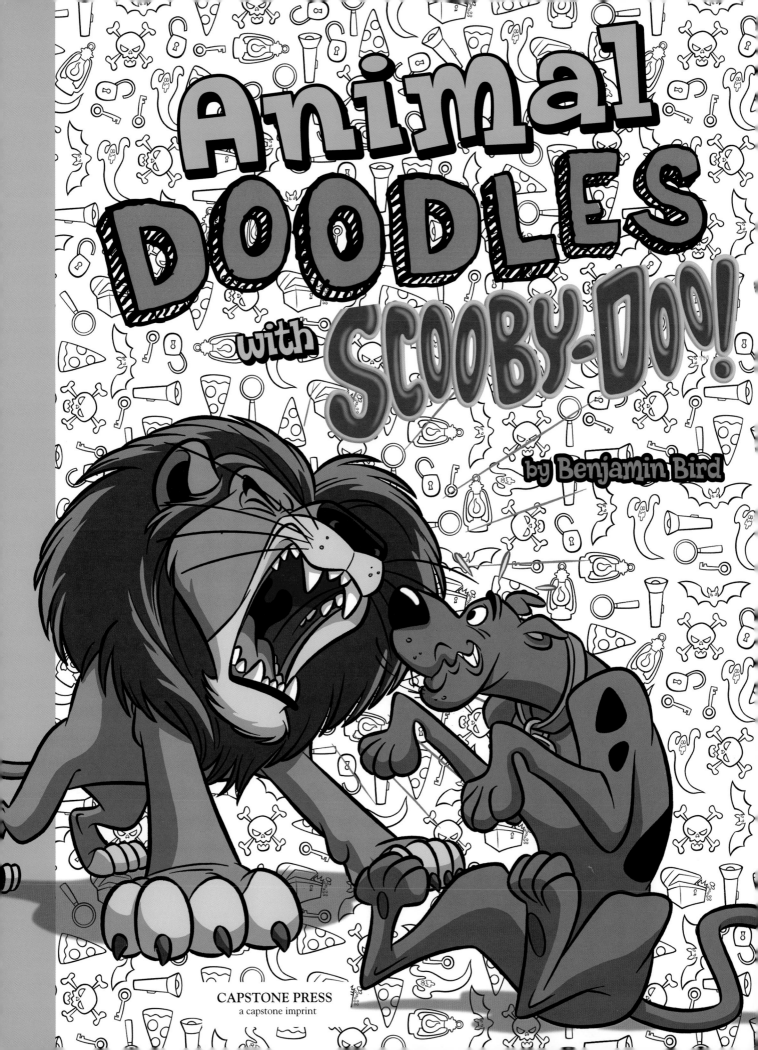

Animal DOODLES
with SCOOBY-DOO!

by Benjamin Bird

CAPSTONE PRESS
a capstone imprint

Scooby-Doodles!
are published in 2017 by Stone Arch Books,
A Capstone Imprint
1710 Roe Crest Drive,
North Mankato, Minnesota 56003
www.mycapstone.com

CAPS38615

Cataloging-in-Publication Data is available on the Library of Congress website.

ISBN: 978-1-5157-3405-5 (hardcover)
ISBN: 978-1-5157-3410-9 (eBook)

Summary: Draw and create ANIMAL doodles with Scooby-Doo!

Designed by Lori Bye

Capstone Studio: Karon Dubke, (supplies) 5; Scott Neely: (sketches) 8-9, 10-11,
12-13, 16-17, 19, 20-21, 23, 25, 27, 29

All other illustrations not listed above are credits to Warner Brothers

TABLE OF CONTENTS

LIKE, HELP, SCOOBS!

Zoinks! Think art is truly terrifying? Well, think again.

Like solving a great mystery, drawing just takes a little planning and practice. In *Animal Doodles with Scooby-Doo!*, you'll discover tools, tips, and tricks to make doodling a totally wild experience.

Use this book for daily doodling fun! In your own sketchbook, follow Scooby and the gang through warm-up exercises, pattern practice, and step-by-step drawing instructions.

You'll unmask your inner artist in no time!

TOOLS

Scooby and the gang need proper tools, like flashlights and magnifying glasses, to solve mysteries. With a few basic tools, you can doodle like a pro!

ERASER

Ruh-roh! Don't fear mistakes. An eraser can solve most problems.

RULER

Even the shakiest hand can draw a straight line with a ruler.

PENCILS

Jinkies! Worried about making mistakes? Sketch outlines of your doodles first. They're great for detailed coloring, too!

FINE-TIP MARKERS

Any great detective knows details matter — the same goes for great doodlers! Use fine-tip, waterproof markers to give your drawings scary-good details.

COLORED MARKERS

Don't get lost in the dark! Brighten up your doodles with multicolored markers.

MEET MYSTERY INC.

SCOOBY-DOO

SKILLS: Loyal; super snout
BIO: This happy-go-lucky hound avoids scary situations at all costs, but he'll do anything for a Scooby Snack!

SHAGGY ROGERS

SKILLS: Lucky; healthy appetite
BIO: This laid-back dude would rather look for grub than search for clues, but he usually finds both!

FRED JONES, JR.

SKILLS: Athletic; charming
BIO: The leader and oldest member of the gang. He's a good sport — and good at them, too!

DAPHNE BLAKE

SKILLS: Brains; beauty
BIO: As a sixteen-year-old fashion queen, Daphne solves her mysteries in style.

VELMA DINKLEY

SKILLS: Clever; highly intelligent
BIO: Although she's the youngest member of Mystery Inc., Velma's an old pro at catching crooks.

GANGWAY!

Wild animals might turn Scooby and Shaggy into scaredy-cats, but have no fear of doodling. Use these warm-ups to let your inner artist ROAR!

In your sketchbook, doodle all of these **DOG TAGS,** and then create some of your own!

In your sketchbook, doodle as many
ANIMAL TEETH
as you can in five minutes!

DISCOVER PATTERNS

To crack a case, great detectives look for patterns of evidence. Doodling patterns — repeating the same design over and over — can help you discover your path to drawing success.

USE THESE SUGGESTIONS TO CREATE YOUR OWN
ANIMAL FOOTPRINT PATTERN!

BUTTERFLIES AND INSECTS!

Scooby-Doo and Shaggy are on a ghost-hunting safari.
Create an animal print pattern for their new outfits!

FIND CLUES

Scooby and the gang focus on finding small clues to solve big mysteries. Grid drawing is a great way to break a large illustration into smaller, more manageable parts.

TOOLS:
Ruler
Pencil
Paper
Fine-tip marker
Eraser

1. Using the ruler and pencil, draw a grid of squares like the one on page 15 (five columns and seven rows).

2. Next, choose a square of Scooby and the seal to draw with the fine-tip marker.

3. Once you've finished drawing one square, start on another. And then another and another!

4. When you've finished drawing all the squares, use the eraser to remove the grid from your Scooby drawing!

RUH-ROH!

How do you close a letter under water?

WITH A SEAL!

FOLLOW LEADS

The Mystery Inc. gang follows a series of leads, or clues, to solve every case. In the pages to come, follow each series of instructions to create groovy drawings.

VELMA

1. With a pencil, lightly outline the main shapes of Velma's body and head.

2. Using the outline as your guide, draw her outfit, including her skirt and shoes. Add her hair and fingers, too!

3. Then, give Velma some details! Add her eyes, glasses, and mouth. Afterward, erase any unnecessary lines and fix any last-minute mistakes.

4. ADD COLOR! Outline your drawing with a fine-tip, black marker. Then use colored markers to bring Velma to life!

JINKIES!

DAPHNE!

Now try your hand at doodling this mystery-soving fashionista! You'll be a pro in four easy steps. Creepers!

1. With a pencil, lightly outline the main shapes of Daphne's body and head.

2. Using the outline as your guide, draw her outfit, including her skirt and shoes. Add her hair and headband, too!

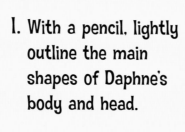

3. Then, give Daphne some details! Add her eyes, eyebrows, and mouth. Afterward, erase any unnecessary lines and fix any last-minute mistakes.

4. ADD COLOR!
Outline your drawing with a fine-tip, black marker. Then use colored markers to bring Daphne to life!

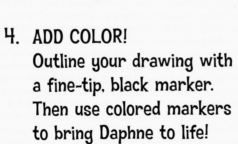

KOALA!

Scooby-Doo isn't scared of every hairy beast. Draw your own cuddly koala in a few simple steps!

1. Lightly sketch the main shapes of the koala with a pencil.

2. Next, add facial features.

3. Then, add details to your outline, such as fur, fingers, and toes.

4. ADD COLOR!
Outline your drawing with a fine-tip, black marker. Then fill in the fur with any color you prefer!

THEN...
Doodle an Australian landscape for your cuddly koala!

ELEPHANT!

What do you give a sick elephant?

PLENTY OF ROOM!

Follow the steps to doodle this enormous elephant in no time!

1. Difficult drawings often begin with simple shapes. To create an elephant, begin by lightly sketching the shapes at left.

2. Next add the basic shapes of the elephant's legs.

3. Then, add facial features and a tail. Erase any unnecessary lines and fix any last-minute mistakes!

4. Outline your drawing with a fine-tip, black marker. Fill in the elephant with any color you prefer!

SKUNK!

Doodle a skunk using the steps on the next page.

How many skunks fit in the
Mystery Machine?

QUITE A PHEW!

1. Begin by outlining the basic shapes of the skunk.

2. Fill in the mouth, eyes, and any other facial features. Once you're finished, erase any unnecessary lines or pencil marks.

3. Then, add details to your outline, such as fur, fingers, and toes.

4. Finally, outline your skunk with a fine-tip marker and color!

T. REX!

Draw your own dinosaur in a few simple steps!

1. First, lightly sketch your T. rex with a pencil. Remember, you will have to erase some lines later on!

2. Next, add details to your dinosaur, such as an eye and razor-sharp teeth.

3. Fill in any last-minute details. Once you're finished, erase any unnecessary lines or pencil marks. Finally, outline your T. rex with a fine-tip marker and color!

THEN . . .
Doodle a prehistoric landscape for your deadly dino!

LION!

Draw your own lion in a few simple steps!

1. Begin any face by identifying the basic shapes, including half circles, ovals, and triangles. Remember: sketch lightly with a pencil at first! You can always erase any unnecessary lines or mistakes later on.

2. Next, use the basic shapes as an outline for the remainder of your drawing. For the lion, add eyes above the nose and a tuft of hair beneath its chin.

3. Fill in the nose, add pupils and any other facial features.

4. Once you're finished, erase any unnecessary lines or pencil marks. Outline your lion with a fine-tip marker and color!

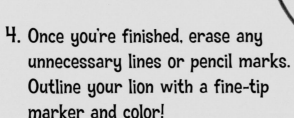

Benjamin Bird

Benjamin Bird is a children's book editor and freelance writer from St. Paul, Minnesota. He has written books about some of today's most popular characters, including Batman, Superman, Wonder Woman, Scooby-Doo, Tom & Jerry, and many more.

Scott Neely

Scott Neely has been a professional illustrator and designer for many years. Since 1999, he's been an official Scooby-Doo and Cartoon Network artist, working on such licensed properties as Dexter's Laboratory, Johnny Bravo, Courage The Cowardly Dog, Powerpuff Girls, and more. He has also worked on Pokemon, Mickey Mouse Clubhouse, My Friends Tigger & Pooh, Handy Manny, Strawberry Shortcake, Bratz, and many other popular characters. He lives in a suburb of Philadelphia and has a scrappy Yorkshire Terrier, Alfie.

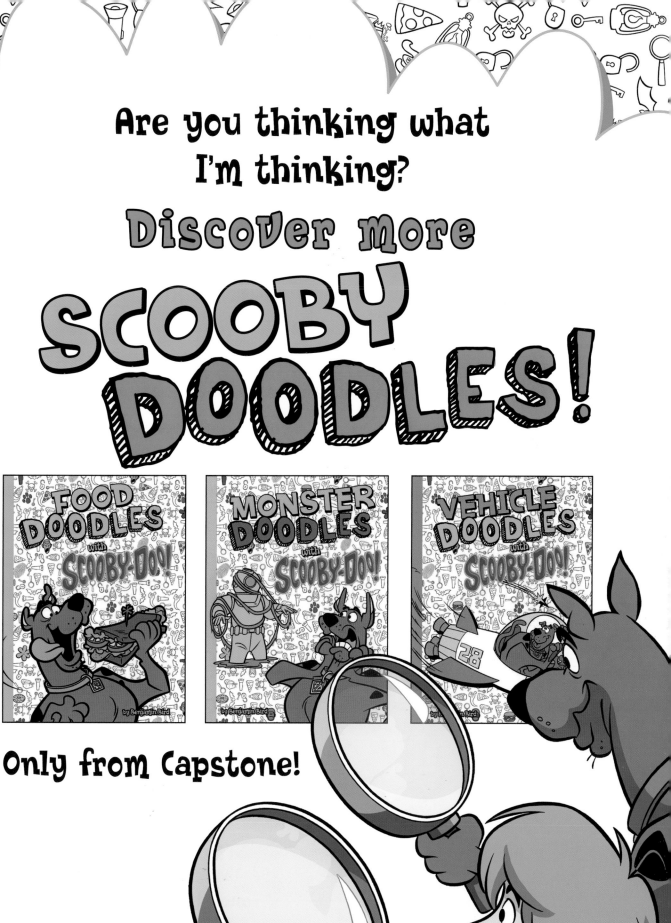